Feelings
and
Emotions

BY KATHY THORNBOROUGH • ILLUSTRATIONS BY KATHLEEN PETELINSEK

The Child's World®

A SPECIAL THANKS TO OUR ADVISERS:
As a member of a deaf family that spans four generations, Kim Bianco Majeri lives, works, and plays amongst the deaf community.

Carmine L. Vozzolo is an educator of children who are deaf and hard of hearing, as well as their families.

PUBLISHED by The Child's World®
1980 Lookout Drive • Mankato, MN 56003-1705
800-599-READ • www.childsworld.com

ACKNOWLEDGMENTS
The Child's World®: Mary Berendes, Publishing Director
The Design Lab: Design
Jody Jensen Shaffer: Editing

PHOTO CREDITS
© 3dv1n/iStock.com: back cover, 15; Alina555/iStock.com: 18; Asier Romero/Shutterstock.com: 8; Diego Cervo/Shutterstock.com: 23; discpicture/Shutterstock.com: 12; drbimages/iStock.com: 22; gjohnstonphoto/iStock.com: 13; Jeanette Dietl/Shutterstock.com: 21; LeventKonuk/iStock.com: 10; maxim ibragimov/Shutterstock.com: cover, 1, 11; PathDoc/Shutterstock.com: 4, 5, 14, 16, 17; pixelbrat/iStock.com: 9; Serhiy Kobyakov/Shutterstock.com: 3; Susii/Shutterstock.com: 19; tarinoel/iStock.com: 6; wavebreakmedia/Shutterstock.com: 7; Yuri_Arcurs/iStock.com: back cover, 20

ISBN 9781626873186
LCCN 2014934486

PRINTED in the United States of America
Mankato, MN
July, 2014
PA02216

NOTE TO PARENTS AND EDUCATORS:

The understanding of any language begins with the acquisition of vocabulary, whether the language is spoken or manual. The books in the Talking Hands series provide readers, both young and old, with a first introduction to basic American Sign Language signs. Combining close photocues and simple, but detailed, line illustrations, children and adults alike can begin the process of learning American Sign Language. Let these books be an introduction to the world of American Sign Language. Most languages have regional dialects and multiple ways of expressing the same thought. This is also true for sign language. We have attempted to use the most common version of the signs for the words in this series. As with any language, the best way to learn is to be taught in person by a frequent user. It is our hope that this series will pique your interest in sign language.

Amazed

Open and close your hands near your face. Repeat.

Another word for amazed is "astonished."

3

Angry

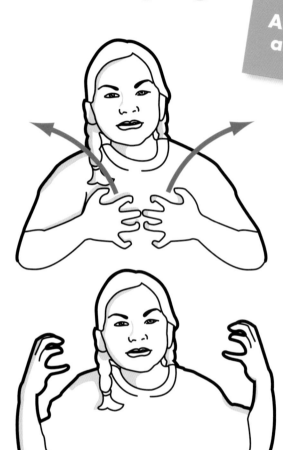

Another word for angry is "mad."

Make claws with your hands.
Start at your belly and pull
outward and upward.

Another word for cranky is "grouchy."

Cranky

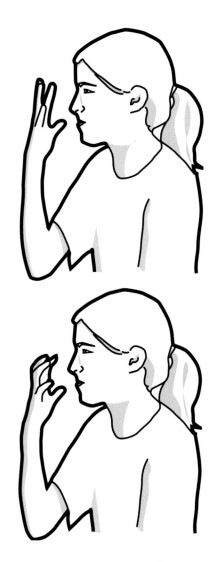

Bend your fingers toward your face.
Repeat.

Defiant

Make a fist facing toward you.
Turn it outward quickly.

Another word for
defiant is "resistant."

Disappointed

Another word for disappointed is "downhearted."

Point to your chin and frown.

7

Disgusted

Make a claw hand. Move as if you are scratching your belly in a circular motion. Make your face as if you are disgusted.

Another word for disgusted is "repelled."

Another word for doubtful is "uncertain."

Doubtful

Bend your fingers toward your face. Repeat.

9

Frustrated

Smack the back of your hand (lightly) into your face twice.

Another word for frustrated is "irked."

Another word for happy is "jolly."

Happy

Place a flat hand on your chest.
Quickly move up, out, and around
in a loop (your palm always
faces your chest). Repeat.

11

Hurt

Another word for hurt is "wounded."

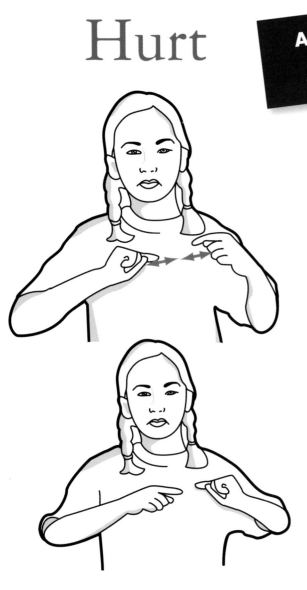

Point two fingers toward each other. Then twist in different directions (if your right hand twists clockwise, your left hand twists counterclockwise).

Proud

Another word for proud is "contented."

Point your thumb at your belly.
Move upward toward your chest.

13

Puzzled

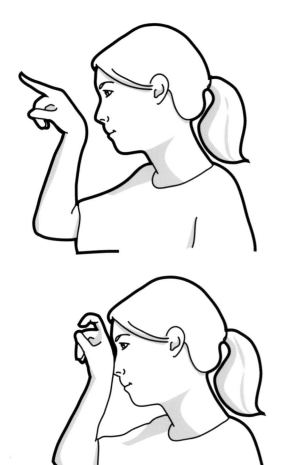

Point outward, then curl
your finger and bring it
to your forehead.

14

Another word for
puzzled is "confused."

Sad

Make a sad face. Place both hands in front of your face and pull down, like tears.

Satisfied

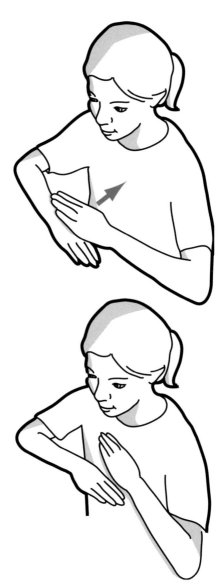

Another word for satisfied is "appeased."

Bring both flat hands in toward your chest at the same time.

Another word for selfish is "greedy."

Selfish

Pull your fingers in as if you are pulling something toward you.

Shy

Twist your bent hand against your cheek.

Another word for shy is "bashful."

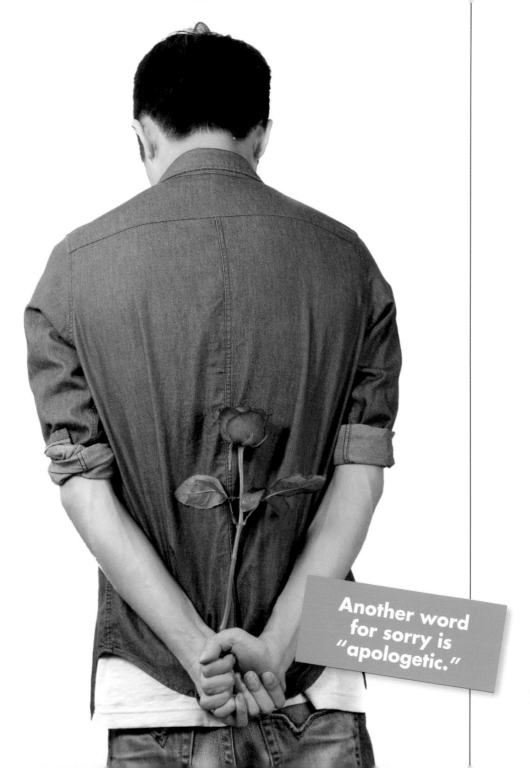

Sorry

Another word for sorry is "apologetic."

Place your fist on your chest. Circle around twice.

19

Thoughtful

Make a loop around your temple area. Repeat.

Another word for thoughtful is "reflective."

Thrilled

Wiggle your fingers on your chest, then bring them up and outward.

Another word for thrilled is "elated."

Upset

Make the "K" sign. Point downward.
Then flop and point upward.

Another word for upset is "agitated."

Another word for worried is "anxious."

Worried

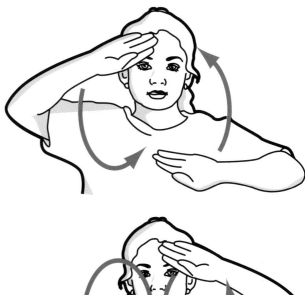

Using your flat hands, make small circles in opposite directions. Move as if you are swatting away worries that are troubling you.

A SPECIAL THANK YOU!

A special thank you to our models from the Program for Children Who are Deaf and Hard of Hearing at the Alexander Graham Bell Elementary School in Chicago, Illinois.

Aroosa loves reading and playing with her sister Aamna. Aroosa's favorite color is red.

Carla enjoys art, as well as all kinds of sports.

Deandre likes playing football and watching NFL games on television.

Destiny enjoys music and dancing. She especially likes learning new things.

Xiomara loves fashion, clothes, and jewelry. She also enjoys music and dancing.

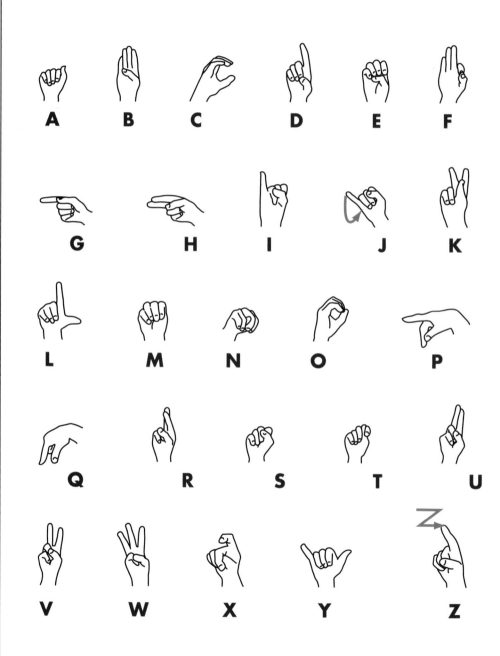